Here is the Night and the Night on the Road

Here is the Night and the Night on the Road

Mónica Gomery

Cooper Dillon

Acknowledgments

A different version of this book's middle section was published as *Of Darkness and Tumbling*, a chapbook from YesYes Books, in fall 2017, and was chosen as a finalist in the YesYes Books 2016 Vinyl 45s Chapbook Contest.

Coma Poems II, V, VIII, and "Visit" appeared in *Hold: a journal*. X was a finalist in the Alexander and Dora Raynes Poetry Competition of Jewish Currents Magazine and appeared in *Urge*, an anthology of this competition. IX, XVIII, and XXV appeared in *Big Big Wednesday*. "The thought of writing a whole letter to you," "key words and small objects," "Questions About Smell," and "Season of Elegy" appeared in *Fog Machine*.

In "Ars Poetica," the phrase "Our Beauty and Terror" comes from Elizabeth Alexander's *The Light Of The World*. The idea of "speaking from our scars not our wounds" comes from Lutheran pastor Nadia Bolz-Weber.

Here is the Night and the Night on the Road
Copyright © 2018 by Mónica Gomery

All rights reserved
First edition
Cooper Dillon Books
San Diego, California
CooperDillon.com

Cover Image by Claire Briguglio (cbriguglio.com)
Interior Design: Adam Deutsch

ISBN-13: 978-1-943899-05-0

Printed in the United States

Table of Contents

TO SAY   1

    THE COMING OF A GREAT SKY   3

THE EXACT THING   11
THE THOUGHT OF WRITING A WHOLE LETTER TO
    YOU   12
QUESTIONS ABOUT SMELL   14
KEY WORDS & SMALL OBJECTS   15
SEASON OF ELEGY   16
SEASON OF ELEGY   17
HOSPICE   18
DEATH IS   20
ELEGY   21
YOU WOULD HAVE   23
ELEGY   25
ELEGY   26
OUR LAST DAY TOGETHER   27
*   28
DAY BURNT THROUGH BY THE BRIGHT OF YOU   29

    COMA   33

    SWEET SONG OF THE EARTH   67

*   69
*   71
ANGER   72
CONFESSION   73
*   74
CONFESSION   75

I say this very quietly   78
Visit   82
*   84
Anger   85
Confession   86
Land   88
The Biggest   89
Spring Song   90
Let Go   92
Elegy   94
Ars Poetica   95

    Gratitude   100

Here is the world; I lost
the world or so I thought.

                                        Cathy Park Hong

To Say

> *to say you loved a person.*
> *to say that person no longer exists.*
>   *Mary Jo Bang*

To say I choose the world, and you in it.
Wide and blasted through
with green,
and bleeding light, I don't
know how else to name it.

To say hard rain, thirsting earth,
the place where your grandmother's
memory drops off.
To dedicate every word to you
to suffocate inside these syllables,
to crawl into the widest sky
to rhyme with hollow, to say thick water,
to say it carves me out of myself,
to say this joy is manic.

To say there are three pronouns
inside of these poems
I, you, and You
but brother is also a pronoun
and earth is somehow all of us.

To say earth is somehow all of us.
To say we grieved your death inseparable
from our grieving for the world.
To rhyme world with brother,
to miss you, to miss you hungrily,
tragically, gratefully, furious.

To lie down beside the fresh earth
of your grave and look up at the willow
at the widest sky
to say this earth is my brother
this brother is my lover
this death is a dream I can't wake from.

To say you loved a person
to wrangle laughter up through the throat
to lean toward the light
to die every day inside of our bodies
and rise every day inside of your memory.

To say you loved a person,
to choose the world
to choose the world,
and you in it.
Wide and blasted through
with green,
and bleeding light, I don't
know how else to say it.

THE COMING OF A GREAT SKY

Because the story itself feels like too much to tell.
Because I've only ever been able to tell it stone,
tell it cold-membraned-over, tell it
with uncrackable walls.
Because I've only ever been able to tell it stone.
Because I don't believe in throwing stones at the page.

The story, the stones, the uncrackable walls.

                              The grieving I so hopelessly small
                                 so clenched in its glue-bubble
                                        of sorrow and ache.
                                    The shameful solitude
                                    of the small grieving I.

A brain is a quilt of echoes.

After death the simplest things become the most confounding—
WHAT DO YOU MEAN no more:
1. your voice
2. your hands
3. the fact of your body upright and alight
4. sorcery of your mind making sauce of our world
5. the fact of your body upright and alight
WHAT DO YOU MEAN cells organs reflexes
6. the fact of your absence.

While the brain is shrinking, where does consciousness go?

Look up at the sky; opposite of the brain.

BRAIN
contours labyrinthine folds
tucked and cabbaged together
circuit systems, nervous systems
rhizomes and sparkplugs

                        SKY
every crevice unruffled and spread, space and the space within space
and diffusion of light, gaping dilated expansive as breath

BOTH
limitless   uncontained   uncontainable

Sky is not the opposite of Brain   where did you go?

Last night I dreamt your aunt died and one of your cousins died too, the one who is not pregnant, and her husband died and so did the husband of the one who is pregnant. And the one who is pregnant was left suddenly alone, and trembling, and the face of the earth full of pathways and clearings was suddenly very, very wide open.

> Because the face of the earth is wide
> and sometimes there is no shade to be found.

> I did not know the edge between me and we.
> How strong or how flimsy that edge.

> A sky big enough to drown us in blueness, a sky
> hot and mean enough to smother you out.

Because there is carbon in the atmosphere.
Swirling us, streaming through, dragging along.
Because it is gathering in increased concentration
bundling itself, generating heat.
Because carbon in our bodies composes 18.5% of human mass.
Crust of earth tumbling stratosphere, rolling our bones.

Because wildfires, sea level rise, tropical drought.

Because carbon is where earth and sky collide.
Because carbon is where the crust of the earth is the same as the crust of our bodies.

You were trying to clasp carbon. Bury it back into the soil. To run it through root beds, to hold it at bay. Scientists call it sequestration. You called it serving the sacred.

Bandits, bioengineers, chestnut farmers, foresters, anti-frackers, herbalists and midwives, green rabbis, your brothers, heirloom-variety gardeners, arborists, economists, embroiderers, senators and chiefs, permaculturists, woody agriculturists, number crunchers, storytellers. Grasping and hopeful. Not nearly everyone, but you were not alone.

This great God of Molecules. This silt in the air.
Patching lacerations. Burning chaos of atmosphere.

Every blade of grass speaking its name back to you.

You didn't know lightning storms shake the midwestern nights. You drank the air sparking electric, said to your brother *I could be ready to die*

How lustrous the light pouring through you.

Boy who felt on behalf of everything feeling. The ability to understand and share the feelings of another. To feel, as in: everything has an experience that is also connected to everything else's experience. A science driven by empathy. His questions: *how does it work, what does it do?* but what he meant was: to take the world, this whole great God Of Molecules, take it all into his sloshy throb and feel what it would feel. Feel what soil feels. Feel what fungi feel. Feel people bumping around inside of him. Sweet barefoot empathy and asking hands, sense of dazzled wholeness in the weaver's loom. To speak in the language of God which is a composite of sentient parts. A boy who walked the world with all his needles pointed upward to the great wide sky and whispering *what shall I do to serve You what shall I do to serve You* and all the while the crashing waves of fear and reverie upon him.

When she met him she felt a new kind of aching. She had not known that love could be the edging up beside a brother. She found herself trying to get back to a womb they had shared somewhere before. The way siblings don't choose one another. The science of empathy. Why are we bound up together? How does it work?

Impossible ecstatic brother she could not *yes* or *no*, she could not *I* or *we* it fully and so they met in the middle place and let their limbs braid seasons.

That evening when they kissed on the couch and he pulled his face away from hers a little so she could look at him and asked *what do you see?* And after she had looked a while she answered *Time.* And he smiled and nodded then, because he knew something about it. She will never know why he nodded that night and what he knew.

The things she does know are not easy to transmit – something about absence, about water and light. Something about what surfaces in a life when trust drops out and the floor of the world is not what she thought it would be

about diffusion of light, gaping dilated expansive as breath

limitless the wound of it   beating   bright

a blazing, burnt-out sky   covered in carbons rolling our bones

like a canopy over us blocking the sun

you are the sun and you are the mind of the sun

the breathlessness of light.

The Exact Thing

> *One day it happens: what you have feared all your life,*
> *the unendurably specific, the exact thing. No matter what*
> *you say or do.*
>   Marie Howe

The brothers are dreaming again
chase scenes, clamoring circus
you on the phone line scratching out
syllables of *ok*

what comes first is love
and what can be built
is built around it

things are not simple
you are not a story

in one moment the fullness
of atoms colliding the day
love swells to fill the hot
wound of a life
there is wind, there is
a precise word for this

in the next moment
the fact of it aches as it
undoes the world

The Thought of Writing a Whole Letter to You

The thought of full sentences.

I unfold your t-shirt.
I take it to the forest.
I cross the road
when the cars are
too close.

I can see your body.
In the absence of your body.
The way planets bump up
against bones and wind-
chimes collide
in your body.

Your voice.
With the moss bedding over
your voice.
Your knuckles. Where bees rest
their soft underbellies.

I have questions about smell.

What the fingers hunt, bunching
the cloth close to the face.
What the lungs learn
when I try to swallow
your t-shirt.

Your t-shirt is not a full sentence.

I have questions
about wind
combing leafless branches.
About the carpet of birchwood
and whether sap carries memory.

I look for you in the spaces
between bodies of trees. The quiet
keen on your lack,
your elbows are loud
in the unseeable air.

We never made the plan
for where we'd meet up
the day the oil runs out.

It's not as simple as ghosts or stars
falling from sockets.
The way autumn tilts
itself from yellow to brown.

Questions About Smell

Someone said — particles. Meaning: there are particles of the dead that remain above ground, traveling among us, and oh I discovered if I press my face into your things I can bury myself, a swell a surge an instance of traveling time. So: do these particles have a hard grip on our world? Are they fighting to stay smoldering here? Someone said — sparks. As in: when you close your eyes and lower your nostrils into the neckline of his sweater which you've been wearing for days, it's the sparks of him firecrackering through you, snap of what he lived for, trace left behind. They told us hearing was the last sense to go so we filled your room with song and whispered permission into your face, unresponsive and shrinking away from us in size but not in beauty. And one night your brother gathered us around your bed and read the lewdest book he could find so we could drench you in laughter. They told us hearing was the last sense to go but now it's smell that persists — sparks or particles, present matter or touchstone of unforgetting. Questions about smell: how inhalation can sift and reorder time, how these smallest doses of you can feel so huge now, smallest doses I cannot touch, fingers too clumsy too full of desire. Instead of touch: consume. Instead of reach for: usher in. I imagine my insides spackled with you, glowing brighter by every breath, fragments of chestnut and cardamom powder, snowflakes and leather, graphite and fragmite and potato eyes. I used to say smell of tree bark and brown sugar. Now I notice also smell of turpentine and littlest sibling. My questions are about time and smell and time and smell and time and smell, one rearranging the other, questions of absence and presence and absence and presence as I take you into me and then let you go, over and over again.

KEY WORDS & SMALL OBJECTS

chipped shells
bits of rock
a tiny dried starfish

sunk
world
bright
gone

hollow
residue

piles assemble themselves
beside your photograph

piles that mean to say:
your silence drowns me
when are you coming to see me
when.

Season of Elegy

The graduate students shuffle their papers. The hungry raccoon is digging for chestnuts. The chestnut trees drink carbon out of the sky. The action-blast trumpets through pixels to say *Come out come out, no pipeline no pipeline, civil disobedience can keep our waters from burning!* The activist schedules her speaking tour. The radio show reports a battle for fracking on the floor of the House. The lightning storm sparks Minnesota. The First Nations alliance issues a statement on sacred water and women's safety as casualties of the pipeline. The urban farmer is digging for garlic. The middle-school yard houses an untended orchard planted a hundred years ago during a public commons initiative. The pear tree grows despite its un-pruning. The banker considers joining the compost collective. The reporter tweets from the rally. The lobbyist for the dairy industry walks her dog on the lake. The police arrest a teenaged boy on a boulevard built along an 1816 treaty line between a native community and a colonial army. The grandmother writes down her recipe. The coalition for clean air drops a banner over the freeway. The energy company raises its prices. The muralist mixes his paint. The filmmaker loads a new reel. The students are digging for soil samples. The geese knit the sky with their callings. The logger takes a second job at an international bank. The badger gets under the fence. The hazelnut trees drink carbon out of the sky.

Season of Elegy

It was summer and then it was fall. The small things were the same as they always were: dozens of subway rides, hundreds of cups of coffee. Each day began swabbed in light and almost imperceptibly the planet kept heating up. The knotweed in the cemetery continued to climb the fence. The trumpet-flowers opened their triumphant mouths, drank the sun, shriveled as the air turned cool. In every single moment of each day and night, every single living thing inhaled and then exhaled, inhaled and then exhaled. We lived like this, breath to breath, as summer came and went, then fall. We opened and closed our hands many times, looking into them, trying to understand what we'd lost. They looked back at us like clouded mirrors, in which we could see the shape of ourselves, could see the blur of your shape rubbed up against them.

How do you get dressed to go watch someone die?

The day is brightening. Somewhere someone is hands-in-the-field, lifting potatoes up into the daylight. Somewhere someone is finishing their cleaning shift before the office fills with suits, last plastic bag knotted, cinched, and tossed into the bin. Somewhere a child is unpeeling wet pajamas from against bashful legs.

We inhale and exhale and ride the subway to the hospital or we walk, we get off the train, we blink and we blink. For a moment we can tell it is a vast woven season, and that everything has always been hooked to everything else. We look down at our hands. We look up at the sky. We walk through the hospital doors which close behind us like a curtain, like quiet.

Hospice

We were
brittle like
ball gowns
built out
of icicles.
We were
slit
curtainless,
bloody.
Everyone treading
carefully but
still too
loud for
us.
We just
stood and
sat by
the bed,
staring
and
breathing
and
waiting
and
holding
and
silent
and
singing
and

hating how
much
love
we had
heaving
inside.

Death is

extraordinary ordinary extraordinary ordinary extraordinary ordinary
extraordinary ordinary extraordinary ordinary extraordinary ordinary
extraordinary ordinary extraordinary ordinary extraordinary ordinary
extraordinary ordinary extraordinary ordinary extraordinary ordinary
extraordinary ordinary extraordinary ordinary extraordinary ordinary
extraordinary ordinary extraordinary ordinary extraordinary ordinary
extraordinary ordinary extraordinary ordinary extraordinary ordinary
extraordinary ordinary extraordinary ordinary extraordinary ordinary
extraordinary ordinary extraordinary ordinary extraordinary ordinary
extraordinary ordinary extraordinary ordinary extraordinary ordinary
extraordinary ordinary extraordinary ordinary extraordinary ordinary
extraordinary ordinary extraordinary ordinary extraordinary ordinary
extraordinary ordinary extraordinary ordinary extraordinary ordinary
extraordinary ordinary extraordinary ordinary extraordinary ordinary
extraordinary ordinary extraordinary ordinary extraordinary ordinary
extraordinary ordinary extraordinary ordinary extraordinary ordinary
extraordinary ordinary extraordinary ordinary extraordinary ordinary
extraordinary ordinary extraordinary ordinary extraordinary ordinary
extraordinary ordinary extraordinary ordinary extraordinary ordinary
extraordinary ordinary extraordinary ordinary extraordinary ordinary
extraordinary ordinary extraordinary ordinary extraordinary ordinary
extraordinary ordinary extraordinary ordinary extraordinary ordinary
extraordinary ordinary extraordinary ordinary extraordinary ordinary
extraordinary ordinary extraordinary ordinary extraordinary ordinary
extraordinary ordinary extraordinary ordinary extraordinary ordinary
extraordinary ordinary extraordinary ordinary extraordinary ordinary
extraordinary ordinary extraordinary ordinary extraordinary ordinary
extraordinary ordinary extraordinary ordinary extraordinary ordinary
extraordinary ordinary extraordinary ordinary extraordinary ordinary
extraordinary ordinary extraordinary ordinary extraordinary ordinary

Elegy

Here's how
I remember it:

balloons
and a banner and
a feeling of great
generosity

a dark room
a two-headed human
in a cloak
playing the guitar
playing the flute
with four hands and
a pile of leaves

and love lifting
her skirts and gathering
us in under them.

I remember
the bright tinsel
Sunday, the arch
of your back strong
and thin in the bed

the sense we
had struck gold.

Walking to the goat shed
at dusk and the steam
lifting off of the milk
in the pail.

I remember
learning to recognize
your handwriting
how small
your letters
could get in direct
proportion to how
wide your amazement.

Scaling the mountain,
in gold and in pine,
the way you always looked
warm enough as winter
arrived.

You wrote me a song
about midwives
and mothers
we went shopping together
for pencils and staplers.

Here's how
I remember it:
we slept
next to the furnace,
we prayed
next to the trees,
we kept
the lights off and lit
candles instead.

You would have

put all of me into your mouth.

That's how it was: the feeling of a great storming mouth
reaching for me pronouncing my name
roving lust lips mouth machine whirring
stroking the air with those ringing teeth
two rows of tuning forks
stuck through your gums.

You whose elbows chimed arias
whose body curved Godward
you with the sweltering gluttonous
mouth
cramming yours, mine, anyone's life into your mouth
craving life's salts.

Sometimes the oxygen pulled up out my throat
like a rope in a borehole. Sometimes I guarded
my breath from you, gathered all my reserves
and would not exhale.

When I asked for quiet or when I asked you for space
your mouth trembled as though I had slapped at it there.
Your mouth that could invent me
and drape me in sweetness, enunciate
small as a seed or as wide
as the world. Tasting the world
and running it
always under
your tongue.

Some days just your shadow could cut my tongue away.

We weren't the first ones to suffer
from hunger while living in excess.
I wasn't the first woman
to guard all my air.

Elegy

I miss the way your eyes could soft the canopy

I miss the way your limbs could rankle any stillness

I miss the touch of you on every green

      the way you wrung the world and fought for it

      the way you were so dire and so gentle

I miss the way you say my name one syllable

      the way you say the world in all its surnames

I miss the way you were a cawing, trumpeting

I miss the hungry parts of you and all the parts that loved me

      the parts that loved me nested into me beside me
      thick with peace and grave with danger
      the tunneling of your blood loudly
      the daffodiling of your hair
      the way your eyes could century what lay before them
      the way prayer tumbled eager from your trying lips

I miss the swarm of you and your small piles

      the way you scrubbed me clean and hollow
      the way your love was steely wool
      grating at me, gutting me
      and polishing me into something better

I miss the way the world fell into you
the way you were the world.

Elegy

The truth is that you were the minute hand of a clock. The truth is that you were going acidic. That you were so often growing new spores. A scrape before scabbing. A wound shining and slightly infected. You were afraid of the things we so often fear: being a monster, being a mouse, choosing the wrong life, not making an impact, not finding love. You ached for attention, hunger launching your bones, tilting your whole body toward whoever could feed you.

You sometimes fell to the ground and beat your fists into your own face. You feared speaking a language that no one else spoke. You feared being told you were in fact crazy. You shook. You hid. You tumbled out your own mouth. You rambled. You saw things. The woods spoke back to you. They will say that you were as big as a planet but you were an ordinary sized person, sometimes smaller. They will say you were as wide as the ocean and sometimes you were. You were a bright trembling surface of water, and every time you came to see me you had a new face.

The truth is that you were a cyclone, you were a flooding, you were a knuckle of carbon hanging high in the sky. The truth is that a person could lose their balance standing too close. Gravitation is movement toward an attractive force at the center. Hold on to your zippers. Hold on to your hat.

Our Last Day Together

> *Can I love someone...and still think/fly?*
> Susan Sontag

Blame is a small bright seed
bedded into the soil of memory.

I said *scarcity*, and you said *abundance!* I said *not in my body*. You said *try*, and I said *I'm so tired.* You said *trust me more,* and I said *give me quiet.* You said *this earth is too lonely, we need one another.* You said *stay with me through summer.* My sentences chipping apart as they parted my lips. I said *you will always be my brother.* I don't remember if I said this out loud.

When you cried it was blustering. You made the sounds of a water-wheel turning. I was asking you to unhatch yourself. I was pushing you back out into the storm. I told you, *I need to walk it alone for a while.* You said, *I know we can do this.* I could see your collarbone quaking. It rose out of your chest, cracking open your skin. *Come on,* you urged, *just stay with me through summer.* I was also crying. I cried the whole time. You were pleading, pitched high, and the wind had begun to enter the room. The wind rising up through the floorboards and shaking the room by its shoulders. Something had changed in the room. Something had entered, a sense of the future.

There is no way to look back on it clean.

Having left you, I am sure
I could have saved you.

*

Come

tonight we will unearth
our dead
listen to their warnings
conjure them by name

Oh earth,

that spins and spins and drowns,
unleash your bone-cut rubies
your crystallized irises
release the kneecaps
softened into burial discs

send up all the trinkets
what garlands the dead

Day burnt through by the bright of you

a day generous with wind and full of fast movement

your mother's voice comes through the phone line
to tell me about holding her husband,
walking the ocean, touching the objects
you loved to touch

the leaves in flashing departure
as they unclasp their hands
from the boughs and free-fall

mostly it's my awareness of your body in space

the way gravity worked on you

the way your hips and your hinges

the way cups lifted up off you collecting the rain

my friend who lost her baby says the closeness is mostly the cellular indivisible connection they shared, she says often when people are talking she thinks to herself *what is going on here?*

a great wave of dead skin
cells shucking off in the night

your brother tells me how strange it is to look at his body and recognize you: his arms sprouting more hair, his wide palmed hands growing rough like your hands

I wish I was dreaming of your wide rough-palmed hands, that they could bloom into flight before me, catbird wings feathered and striped at the ends of your arms

wind on my eyelashes
proof of being alive

the way it is your body
moving through my body when
I move my body

everything is a promise I intend to keep

that word *flight*, these dreamless cookbooks
the body crushing itself against its own hunger
the blood behind my eyes growing louder

the wind is swift on the face of the pond and the waves look like letters in cursive, and I wish I was dreaming of your hands scripting me letters

autumn lapping the edges of winter
branches fluttering their fingers back at me

a promise

quieting all the parts of the house you once folded your limbs into, darkness comes early

she looks into my eyes in front of the altar of her father and says *you can find another lover, I lost my father, there is no one else to fill his shoes.* And I say *es tu carne y hueso*, even though what I mean is *how could you say that to me*, even though what I mean is *you're right*

this small selfish grief this private metropolis

what exactly is an angel, a ghost, a misfit, a miracle, a lover, matter or memory?

what exactly is this light slicing into everything sideways?

every memory I have of you sounds like *I'm yours* but I never said it

and what is a promise

I intend to keep

COMA

Did you expect a different grace from the world?

Akilah Oliver

I.

There's nothing unique about it: collisions
in darkness. Abrupt and senseless loss.

The unfixable thing held up
against the light of day, rotating it
in my hands.
Unsure if it is filtering light
or producing light.

The summer was sat between phases of you
       axon, neuron
       bloodpuzzle
       quick breathing

Unsure if my singing is rung in your eardrum
or hollowed out by the spoon of my wanting.

II.

Here are your bones in the middle of the road. Here are your bones in the seat next to mine. Here is the car and the skeleton of the car, here is the night and the night rising up over the car. Here is the elk here are its muscles here are the veins in its muscular neck here is the elk in the middle of the road here are your bones in the road. Here is your brother sitting beside me on the stoop in the night, rolling cigarettes, rolling memories of you into cigarettes and sending them out into the city ash-white. Here is your brother in the seat next to mine. On the stoop, rolling cigarettes, rolling your bones into cigarettes. Here is the man driving the truck, cutting his path into the night, foot on the pedal, going the speed limit. Here is the night and the night on the road, here is the sky over the road, here are your bones chandeliering the sky, your bones white and sharp in the sky above the car above the road in the night. Here are your brother's hands on the wheel, they look like your hands, lanky fingered but his nail beds are squared and yours more like raindrops, here are his hands on the wheel and here is the road and your bones in the road. You are lying in the road looking up into the night, your sharp white bones rotating slowly against the black curtain of sky, there is a light pouring through and the whites of your eyes and you are drinking the light with your eyes. Here is the truck, the man driving the truck, cutting his path into the night, here is the singing alive in your car, the sound of two brothers singing, the song is not rising, it stays inside the car, bumping the walls, growing in volume. Here is the elk in the road with eyes looking toward you, eyes pouring with light, and you in the car, or lying down in the road, you singing with your brother in the seat next to mine, rolling your bones into cigarette smoke, you rolling closer in the car toward the man cutting his path into the night and the sky pouring light and the elk in the road watching for you.

III.

V asks what it feels like to touch you. I talk about the you but not you: temperatures of stillness, arm hair and sweat beads and the lattice of scabs etched across. How we clasp to meet your clasp, how we kiss along the exposed parts. The night I discover I can smell your armpits, warm scent of distress unclaimed by hospital. How I like to cup my palms over your kneecaps, beard rough and growing, toenails turning talon. As I tell her, I wonder who I am talking about.

I don't tell how it hurts to look at herb beds, mid-summer shooting up an onion stalk or diffusing soft tufts of dill. I don't tell how it hurts to sleep so I stay awake asking the night.

All I can feel is the you-hole, the place where you aren't. I can feel its perimeter, can press my body into the curve. If I want to, I can fill a pitcher with shimmering light and tip it into the you-shaped relief. The light pools in, swirls for a moment then begins to seep out the edges, corroding container and shape. The light trickles then heaves as it moves, as it drains and invades the scarred earth that surrounds it.

IV.

In this room there are moon boots. There are panels of white, blue and grey-blue and grey-white. In this room a fan runs all day and all night. In this room there are trays on wheels, oxygen in a tube, things that measure things that drip things that pinch things that store what measures pinches drips. In this room we hand-sanitize, we hands on your arms, we try to unclench your hands. In this room respiratory therapy occupational therapy physical therapy. In this room prick for blood sugar squeeze for blood pressure lift for wiping twist for tendon support. In this room you wear inflatable moon boots and the bone of your skull has been partly removed. In this room we tuck prayer fringes into your fist. In this room we framed your portrait, the one R flecked in gold after the crash. In this room I find the smell of your cheek where beard and not-bearded skin intersect and I'm certain, for a moment, it's really you in the bed. In this room I tell your mother how I used to describe the smell of you as tree bark and brown sugar. I tell your father how we listened to Sam K's song on our first night together. In this room everything is the color of ice except for the infectious-waste basket, which is the color of bloodshot. In this room cold kisses your face, your lungs are infected. In this room dressing gown. In this room furrowed brow. In this room eyelids fluttering. In this room I watched your brother cry with his head in his hands. I watched your mom meditate with her palms open wide. In this room strangers say your name like they know you. Your pupils rest like mismatched marbles in this room.

V.

Whether to grieve or whether to pray, trying to clasp hope to my throat like cooling beads on a thread. Try to shape my mouth into *please* but it comes out looking like *you-hole*, sounding like absence already. My eyes widen every time your mother whispers her edges. Her prayer pokes up through white panels in the hospital room.

Coma is an open space. You can try to fit your hope inside it. Space is there for what you want to put. Consider loss, consider miracle. An open space means not that anything could happen. It means we don't know what's happening. Hope is a muscle the size of your brain. The prayer does not whisper to me.

The whole world is collision. Wind combing a tree. Voice invading a skull. Eyes that slap onto a body unwilling. The whole world is wet. Breath barreling into a red leather throat. Wooden banister remembering rainfall.

You are releasing yourself back into the world, like intravenous but in the other direction. I am growing my hair out toward you. We're both made of genetic materials shining and dying.

VI.

You would make words with me. Take road-sign, re-scramble, say *guess what I'm thinking.* A dark car full of talking. *Birdbeard, breadlungs.* Your car with the one red door, rod and piston. Red door opening out onto ocean and other calamities of nature. V told me you kept the car to get to me. Enduring the upkeep and unresolved odors. It broke down after our last drive together.

Consider loss, consider miracle.

Just now sitting here in a tunnel of sunlight and lakeface and hospital feet an old man stops, says to me *Another nice day, haven't had one since the fourth of July,* I say *It's gorgeous* but it comes out the shape of indifference and he says *I heard it was sixty-one dollars to see Bob Dylan,* shrugs, shuffles off.

If I squint both my eyes I can sift out the static and find you in every happen of day.

VII.

It appears you are suffering. It appears you are resting. It appears you are actively dying. It appears you are fighting to live.

Here is your brain swelled up so big they think it will shatter your head. They cut away at the skull to make room for the swelling. They call it a Bone Flap. They leave the flap in a freezer and lay a washcloth over your forehead. We can lift it away with our hands to find thin skin layered over a cavity. It's your brain there on the other side of a curtain. At first it was flush with your forehead, but now your brain is receding and here is a trench caving into your skull.

The trouble with love is brittle and snappable bodies.
The trouble with love is gravel, antlers, and steel.

VIII.

Here is the moment before collision, quiet and floating like a breadcrumb in water, like a worm on the line. Suspension like that. A dangled muted moment embarking on nothing at all before the weight of everything comes headlighting into it. Here is the road and here is the night and the night rising up over the car. Here is the cross-latch of headlights that don't meet in the middle, here is the stillness of lamp-eyes low buzzing, here is the inhale of moment. This is the last moment structurally sound, the last breath you took clear of brainblood or hospital stench. Here is the dark forest teeming with eyes, writhing with predators watching. Here is the inhale of moment. Your brother says that something sank down over the interior of the car in that moment. Call it adrenaline, he says, call it the presence of angels, call it cotton balls sticking to the molecules between things. Here is the road and here is the night and the night rising up over the car. Here is the moment embarking on nothing at all before the weight of everything comes headlighting into it. Here is the witness of shadow and mole, of hairy white asters and green-headed coneflowers, of owl-eyes clicking through darkness. Here is Wisconsin, stalking the night, here is the stillness at the edge of the road, here is a place we never thought we would leak from, and here is the inhale of moment. Here is the moment before collision, quiet and floating like a breadcrumb in water. Here are cotton balls sticking to the molecules between things. Here is the presence of angels. Here is the elk who has bounded over the edge of the road and stops for a moment at the edge of the forest to blink, suspension like that, and here is the moment before collision, and here is the inhale of moment, and here is the last moment before everything, everything, here is the last.

IX.

Bearded men echo you. Baby born with a tousle of hair thick and black. Wanderer, you have been out there for days that bleed into weeks. You will return wizened and new. An old man pulls his car into the lot, flips off the engine, his face is your face but covered in age. Strangers tell me *I will pray for him.* One stumbles, says *pray, I mean wish.*

I imagine the streams and ravines all barreling toward you, the water organizing itself and charging the changed world. *You have this on your side, this on your side,* waters whispering *brother, brother,* rush and roar forth, water carving the face of the mountain on its way down to you. Fill you up with the sound of waters careening, the entropy inevitable of what fluid moves. I pick up the phone, call R: *It is so good you are trusting gravity,* she reminds me, *the Great Lakes are old water, ancient, also children of glaciers.*

X.

Rain is a yes that washes the world. Yes smudging yes clean with its hope. Lightning storm yeses me awake in the night. Then the yes cascades over the house, around the house, cocooning the house in yes, sound of yes rushing, of yes sliding along.

They say you had a shearing injury. Diffuse Axonal, brain cells froze with the shaking. This means neurons everywhere with x's for eyes. They tell us you can't restore what's died off in your brain. No cables for jumping the wreck. That you will have to train new neural pathways into your life like a miner heaving open the earth rock by rock. Like a pianist tunneling sound into the world key by key.

Tonight the hard rains wake me, beating the house in wet rhythms. You are five blocks away, ragged breaths in a rotating bed. The rain singing your night, its blunt melody falling, falling into your mind.

I put my body in the hospital pool, let my strength pull me across. I call R to tell her it has been a day of water. She says *this is the deep within us calling out to the deep within others. Water is a good messenger, everything moves fast along its silver threading.*

I bless your brain with the seeping of water, that it pour forth into new pipelines when it's time, that we will one day see you afloat in a body of water, smiling, suspended, drunk with the love of return.

XI.

Your parents write updates like weather reports: *Mild stirs overnight but calm today. Afternoon restful with storms overnight.* Yesterday we all pledged ourselves to one another. I touched as many surfaces of you as the tubes and the gown would allow, fussing your eyebrows, palming your chin. Now the day ticks out its strange minutes against your body and mine.

P leaves me a message: *I'm trying to feel your pain.* I am moved and confused. Birds fly through the panels, the woods spell your name in green wailing. There are wars and acquittals, the world is huge, I feel swallowed. The girl bagging groceries asks *how is your friend?* I say *it's going to be a very slow recovery.* She says *that's how real healing happens.*

This is me, mangled with wildflowers, shot through with light. This is my hummingbird heart needled and winged, fishing-wire threaded and strung. This is me, tangle of echoes, trying to peer into the you-hole.

Glass shards kaleidescoping wildflowers.

XII.

Last thing you ever said to me was *Can I send you a postcard.* Actually, the last thing you ever said to me was written, it was *ziggens,* and then you signed your name. It's too late to request clarification.

I laid my hand on the gash in the road but that scar is a metaphor not the place where you left us.

XIII.

Your name is my heartbeat knocking against me.

I dream your car hit six birds
in the night instead of spinning into the truck.
One bird for every day of the week
and no bird for Shabbat. The point of collision
is a black pop of feathers, the way a child or
a cartoonist might draw fireworks with a crayon. A soft,
almost celebratory eruption. Bird bones twiggy not quite
translucent yield to the metal then splinter
apart. The car is undented but suddenly
airborne, lifting itself over shadowy tree line, pumping
and flapping with invisible wings. You and your brother

joyously singing,
rising, rising up, your eyes
in the darkness
white moons climbing bright.

XIV.

They say you had a shearing injury. Diffuse Axonal. This means the road thrashed you into a slumber. Means you got no lullaby the night the shards erupted your singing. This means wildflowers speckled in blood.

I lie awake holding your hand in that moment before elk before spinning and slamming, I lie awake willing myself onto the scene.

Minutes pour forth into minutes.

I have taken all of my brothers to the hospital: The one who drank himself to the margin of his life and mine. The one who suddenly seizured crossing between rooftops. The one who threatened to choke his own breath. Now you, my sung secret brother, the one who offered his hand and I gasped at it, unready. The one who is foxsong and all kinds of endless.

I wonder if the clock will always talk to me saying: *you have to choose, sister.* The clock calls me sister even though we're not siblings. It's condescending. I call you brother even though we were lovers. It's confusing, I know. Come home, foxsong. The shards of you in the night.

XV.

When I feel you I feel you suddenly,
and pressed up against me.

Like it was when we took off
all the impediments except for our skin

and got as close as we could without
getting hurt. It's like that now

only different. A shadow
pressing weight onto my body,

dropping keys into my mouth.
And anyhow, we did get hurt,

didn't we.
When I feel you

you are bent-faced and toothy,
always balming the gasp

with inaudible laughter,
or you slide the side of your thigh

up beside mine or run a quick finger
through my greasy hair.

You catch me picking my nose.
You catch me bad nutrition.

Or imagining the next great love of my life
when I'm supposed to be praying for you.

Oh, V writes to me, *I think it's ok if we SCREAM, I think he would want our fists plugging*

the soil and SCREAMING the suffering earth.

XVI.

Tonight we decide to go in pairs into the room and your mother turns to me, says *will you be my partner?* In the room you are wringing your arms inward and heart tachychardic. You are flinching and twisting your mouth, muscles buckle and warp, you are firing synapses and heavy with sweating. One of us takes your stiff yellow feet into our hands. One of us tenders a song at the side of your face. Your lips grow thrush from their creases, clamping white patches of fungus. I am afraid to touch my lips to your lips. I am singing, your mother is singing. Your mother dignified in her faith and her fear. It is summer in Minnesota and it takes hours for the sun to come down.

I dream of a hospital room with three beds pressed together. Your brother in one, you in the other, and me in a bed between both of you. They need to do tests on your brother, trying to sedate him, for some genetic suspicion they have. He keeps almost going under then waking again. You are curled fetal and your eyes slam suddenly open. Huge eyes wet with fear. I take both of your hands into my hands. I start talking, I'm startled, I'm trying to calm you. You're up out of the bed, bending your knees over and over, and scanning the room for the exit.

When I wake I tell your brother who says he dreamt you started snoring so he started screaming and then you woke up. I tell your father who says last night you opened one eyelid, the pupil resting beneath it a bead rolling away.

XVII.

Sitting beside you your eyelids flicker and spark. Your lips fidget and sputter. Sometimes your brain fires off the signal to yawn and you yawn. Only your left eye floats open. Sometimes I think you are looking at me, something about coming home calling out from your eye, something about suffering or distance or fear. You are soaking the bed with your sweat. I try to fit myself into that sliver of eye, try to stand in the path of your pupil, try to offer some texture of faith.

J calls and says, *Take me into his room with you. We're in there together now, we don't even have to face him. Let's just face the wall. We can hear him breathing, and my hand is touching your hand, maybe just my pinkie, I'm right there beside you, and he is there breathing behind us. Now I'll turn around to look at him, you keep facing the wall. We are in here together, here in his room, there is nothing else going on anywhere except this.*

XVIII.

Consider the gash in the road.

The car you were driving is now in Wisconsin. The road that thrashed you is still in Wisconsin. The farm where you were working is on Deer Road in Minnesota. First you were taken to a hospital in Ironwood, Michigan and then you were transported. The helicopter flew over a scalloped edge of Lake Superior before it brought you to this room. The man driving the truck came from Ottawa. He was driving the speed limit. You and your brother were driving home to Philadelphia. There is no information on the elk in the road other than your brother's memory of antlers throbbing the headlights. Apparently there was no carcass found at the scene.

I look up the man driving the truck and find his posting on linkedin.com, and I stare and I stare at the picture. Trying to carve his face into the night. He knows the texture of darkness you were driving into. He was there. I tell your mother I'd like to write him a letter. He was taken to the hospital and went home the next day. I want to ask him what did it look like in that moment of impact and what did it look like in the moments after that. What did it look like inside him, and has he retold the story.

These are not a set of symbols. They mean exactly what they say. There is a road in rural Wisconsin. A two-lane highway cutting through forest. It was built between 1919 and 1926. I look this all up, gathering clues for some meaning I can't grasp in my hand. There are tall grasses, there are wildflowers, and there was an elk waiting at the edge of the trees. This land was Dakota, Ojibwe and Menominee, before the French brought over guns to trade and treaties to be broken, before the blood shed for territory and fur, the cavalries, the Indian Removal Act.

There were two brothers driving a car in the night. They had no hereditary relationship to the land of Wisconsin. They came dragging their own lands through this land—the echoes of Vilna and Kiev, seed potatoes dug out of Poland, the dusty red mountains rising up between Russia and Central Asia. Dispossessed lands, from which their people have fled. Dragging their dust through the dust of this Midwestern road.

The brothers were guests on a chestnut farm, studying carbons and trees, trying to slow down the heat. In their car, two large coolers containing soil samples to take back to the lab in Connecticut.

I am not allowed to contact the man on the road driving the truck, the other inhabitant of antlers and headlights. We share the shape of a memory, the shape of a night at the edge of mortality, and the distance between us is non-negotiable. It is legally fraught to inquire about a texture of darkness.

The trouble with collision is how it slams us together. Everyone in this story was between one place and the next. I want to ask him where he was going, traveling west on some business of his own. Though I know he was alone in the truck, I want to ask him who traveled with him. The trouble with story is that each person contains multiple people. Each of us dragging our ancestors along. Carrying our many homes pressed up against us. There were not only three men and an elk in the night. There was already blood on the road.

XIX.

Minutes pour forth into minutes.
Brain atrophies into hope.

The elk throbbing the headlights.
The brothers collapsing with beauty into their song.

Here is your brain shrinking in size.
Here is the muscle of hope yielding to collision.

The trouble with love is you are neither dead nor alive.

XX.

Today rain falls all day but we bleed upward into the light. I am folding and unfolding the story of us, sliding seashells and bits of glass into its cloth. Whether to grieve or whether to pray. Mullen and horsehair at the edge of the water.

The load of your absence weighs nothing, you know. It is easy to hold your belongings, arrange them by size, assemble them in taxis, subway cars, airplanes, backseats, and trunks. The summer is spent packing and unpacking bags, lifting our bodies across linoleum floors. The objects are easy to grip and not lose.

The burden is the sound of your voice falling away. Summer is spent flipping your cramped handwritten pages, the boxes of acorns and stones you've assembled, the trail of recordings encrypted onto my phone.

It will take the whole of my life to describe the ache of this love, not longing, not romance, I mean the way it crashes its waves up against me no warning. I mean it is drenching me, running in turrets and carving me channels. I lie down on the shore and let it thrash at me there. I know the sky is a glass vault held over us. Summer is spent at the shore of this loving, at the foot of the bed, in this rotating room with the moon boots.

I am the dream of fingertips falling like rain over your skin.
I etched your silhouette back onto the road.

XXI.

Every minute without use dwindles the brain. The brain unhooks itself over and over. The brain peels away from us, shrinking in size. Every day makes it harder to come back from the distance. The trouble with coma is we can't intervene. One night your eye opens. One day your lips quiver. The brain stutters its code. Some days you lie perfectly still under a blanket of medicine. Some days it's like planets erupt through your body, a chaos of signals and storms.

XXII.

The trouble with time is the tired hours. They expand in heat and roll like beads over my shoulders. B takes me into her arms and it feels like plastic embracing plastic. It has an unfamiliar facial expression. I mean that the embrace makes a facial expression. It has its own face. The face is tired, not porous. The face is blasted out, a bullet-shell, the shell of a car or the shell of a crumpled beer can disguised as the shell of a car. This face is selfish and guileless and burning with sadness. *Loss is old,* says B, *but it's new every time.* She is smiling and suddenly crying, the tears drop off in plastic beads from her childhood face.

Tonight everything rolls, nothing chips or shatters, nothing is asking for your alertness or for your hand on your heart or your hands on the wheel or your brother's hands. In the room rotating against the dark night I kissed the hairs between your knuckles and tried to imagine your hips under the gown. I was tired as soon as I walked into the room and I was tired still when I left.

Here is the moment I swallowed your breath in my mouth. Your foxsong blinked off of the sky. The small bonfire I tended inside your cabin. Here are the woods we held onto for years, and that spot on the rock where the coyote stalked past us.

The trouble with memory is the tumbling forth.

XXIII.

Before the collision your eyes were all over this land. Red fox and hawk, red silt of ore. White spruce, black spruce, balsam and hemlock. I never thought I'd get intimate with Minnesota. When I met you, your beard was sparking and foaming. The trouble with collision is we never know which intimacies await us.

In Duluth I find a feather on the sidewalk every few blocks. We are far north here, leaning hard into thick furrows and forests, wide waters green velvets, a quiet cast out with no echo.

This place is not your home or my home. We rest here in its holding ground, cupped by its palm, edged in by the rocks on the lake. Everything I try to learn of it incomplete with the eyes of a visitor. Distant and crazed with the question of coma. Whether to grieve or to pray. Every clue I scratch at does not reveal you. This land drenched in industry, paper mills, ore mines. This land drenched in lake and the iron of blood. The war that drove out the Dakota from Minnesota happened all over this land. The gash in the road.

XXIV.

The trouble with coma is time halts and stammers.
The trouble with coma is time accrues story.

I remember the first time you went away: three months, it was spring, when you returned the air was dense, Manhattan had on all its lights and we sat passing the season between our faces until you said *can we touch?* and we quickly pressed together our hands, too quick for me. We were underwater, caught in the light-stream moving downwards towards us and everything gave off the glow and the lack of control.

The trouble with love is time bends itself forward.
The trouble with love is kinds of collision.

Here is a memory. Roads between mountains. Pizza. Beer. You start sneezing. Patchy night-eyes. Knees ringing. Terrance McKenna. Tomato sauce. You said, *people need medium-sized truths.* I said, *this ink-ribbon of night.* You said, *this heating up planet.* I said, *I love all of your elbows.* You said, *you are life-long material.* I think, for a moment, back on the road, we both fell asleep with you at the wheel, but everything stayed tightly together, stitched up and stacked between mountains, no loose thread for pulling, no unraveling edge of the night, and a split second later we were awake, our lives two small wounds scraped from the air, oxygen thrumming, the *I love you* of darkness and tumbling forth.

The trouble with memory is the tumbling forth.

What do you mean I may never sit beside you again, shoulders pressing together, passing the season, or you looking at me saying my name in one syllable. I saw a woman with no hair walking the surf. I saw a man with complete aphasia smiling slow and huge after they unhooked his brain. I can sometimes intuit a feeling of unfolding infinity. I can sometimes sense just how ok it will be. Or I want to be better because I am sitting beside you and I want to fill up the world with my better, cram the edges with sourdough, poems, fruit-trees and small pocket-bells.

What do you mean no more charts drawn by your hand, no more listening as you narrate the growth of the forest. What do you mean you did all you could do, cramming your light into the world. What do you mean about that. And what do you mean about pressers, painkillers, about catheters, brain scans, about secretions and storms. What do these things have to do with the boy who lives inside his body like a stork wearing sequins? What do you mean about your stolen shape, the wound in the world, the white sky that says nothing.

The trouble with coma is it's not a story.

It's more like a long day with no talking, everything keeps on breathing, I mean that *everything* is breathing, and nothing makes sense. I wear your shadow under my clothes and when the rainstorm hurries everyone else off the beach I get into the water undressed, I slap at the waves and I rage at the force of this broken summer. And somewhere nearby you sigh and roll toward the next cliff of your dreaming.

XXV.

I want to say nothing is without context. I want to say that all land is stained and all roads are haunted. All collisions are echoes of other collisions. There will be a predicted 33,000 deaths by automobile accident this year. I look this up on your father's phone while they sponge-bathe and turn you in the rotating bed.

I am trying to understand this violence that shattered its way through your life and mine, in relation to other kinds of violence. I'm trying to make sense of this thrashing and loss in a world woven entirely out of thrashing and loss. A world barraged by calamity and calamity's cousin — bright light.

Here is collision, echo of colonization. Echo of climate foreboding, echo of two large coolers that burst through the glass at the moment of crashing. Collision echoing brothers, echo the man driving the truck. It echoes me with the silence of its unknowable story. Collision echoes with guesting, echoes dispossession, echoes the laying of asphalt. The laying of asphalt over the forest between 1919 and 1926, a violence whose echo throbs the land and I'll never know what it sounds like.

Here is the boy neither dead nor alive, and the trouble with love might be asphalt.

The way *living* is a small verb for this throbbing we do.

XXVI.

The trouble with love is bone, glass, and bacteria.
The trouble with love is the distance between cities.

In high school my favorite movie was Hable Con Ella by Pedro Almodóvar. I liked the longing. Two women in comas and the men who love them. Hinged between living and not, status of surviving or being survived. I cannot believe this is our life.

The trouble with memory is everything stories.
Everything slips into dimension of told.

I remember a rainy afternoon in the woods, all that moss holding our weight, your face appearing over me against a dark canopy. You felt woven in with all the wild aliveness and I wondered if we were welcome. We tested out being noisy. Let our elbows and thighs stain sweetly and soil.

The trouble with love is it's sticky and thirsty.
The trouble with love is kinds of collision.

On the bus I play a game. If I throw my attention on it at the right angle, anything I look at is you. Traffic cone. Porta-potty. Migrating geese. Tree-line. Road-markings. Shatter of sunset colliding the median. The engine thrums onward, the bus shimmies and sways and my sense of safety spills into you, spills into sunset, coming apart in the chorus of molecules, coming apart in the you on the road. Shatter of glass kaleidescoping the wildflowers. If I throw my attention on it, anything I look at is you. The bus threw its back out. The driver is a doctor. Hope is a muscle the size of your brain.

The trouble with coma is nothing happens at all.

I don't know how else to tell anyone that you begged me to save your life, because they pounce too fast on *thiswasn'tyourfault* but I know what you were asking when you said *staywithmethroughsummer* and the page in your journal reads *toorealtoosoon*. Now I feel you spinning the wheels of this bus saying *noturningback*.

XXVII.

Words dissolve all around us. Rugged cliffs inside us drop out suddenly into ravines. Gauged places where blood used to move like a river now thunk like an echo. Beauty feels more possible now. Becoming un-shy feels possible now. Your mother says we can be fearless now.

The thrum of the forest rises to meet me. The shadows of canopy lifting. Cut of sunlight bedded in pine needles, bedded over by the cautious hoof of a deer. The rabbits make cluster and circle, the owl tilts a wing.

I don't know how to pray but I imagine this land claiming you now, whether you live or you die.

Yarrow, milkweed, wild raspberry claiming you. The dragonflies claim you.

XXVIII.

Rain is a yes and we bleed upward to meet it. Something will grow here. Wildflowers, glass.

I miss you I love you what happened.

SWEET SONG OF THE EARTH

I was so unprepared for the earth's
grace as it disintegrated beneath me

> Akilah Oliver

*

it closes its eyes, the NO.
Almost gets me
-
to believe it
I mean I do believe it:
NOT. NOT THIS.
NO.

Trunked-up and strong in its
NO BONES
a wall rising over a cliff
undone before it is built

then built, built again
all the while snowing its
NO SNOW
and pushing its biceps of NO
its rattling head
like marring the sky in a
NO CONSTELLATION
like a stopper of NO
affixed to a glass vial
containing the galaxy
swirling delivering
breeding stardust and time

the NO
having its tantrum
the NO tight in its jaw
pounding its pepper-fists
into a universe
into a universe
that murmurs
mmhmm.

*

Come
tonight we will unearth
our dead
listen to their warnings
conjure them by name

Oh earth,

that fills and fills and drains
that pulps us through the sieve of loss
unlanguable earth but loss
and anthill mole claw hoof of deer
release the darkest coins
of what remains
and take us home

Anger

The smiling is starting again.

Put the smiling away.

There are people everywhere (teeth).

Put the smiling away.

Take those wide eyes and bury them somewhere.

Put the smiling away please put away those wide eyes.

Do not ask me to tell ~~you~~
do not sing his bright song
~~you~~ do not know what his skin
spoke in the mornings
~~you~~ are not asking the earth
to cough up its riches

please get control of ~~your~~ teeth.

Oh, forgive me, did ~~you~~ want me not burning, not repelled by ~~your~~ heartbeat?

Were ~~you~~ expecting some gentle and generous wound ~~you~~ could swallow?

The way I commemorate him might make ~~you~~ better

~~your~~ heartbeat offends me
~~your~~ wide stifling eyes.

There are only three pronouns inside of these poems.

Get out of my elegy.

Confession

Basically she
is keeping me earthbound,
she blonde where your darkness
took sprout, she
masculine in the places
your feminine lustered.

Basically she is alive
and you are dead and
she is about sweat, salt and matter
and you are about diffusion,
devotion, and arc of air
slipping over
the hawk's wing.

Basically she is
the hard syllables
of my name the clang
of metal on glass and you
are the thrum of this Sunday
carving white afternoon light

over and through us.

*

How every day I am working to choose which world to inhabit. How firsts feel like fists falling over me everywhere. First blink of the day. First bird of the morning. Straining into a world where you are no longer, listening for the fever of you against air and light. In my bed is your shirt and at night I roll toward it. How having a body is the possibility of throwing myself off of something moving.

*

My teacher tells me that her religious life often falls apart when she needs it the most. In synagogue the prayers bounce off of me like pellets. At home a thin veil. Autumn pulps the night. There is nowhere to be but inside this blanket of grief.

A friend tells me about the indie-gogo campaign for the people who want to inoculate corpses with mushrooms to eat through the toxins and decompose faster.

The poet peels back her eyelids, unclips her mouth and begins to describe worms, ants, and appetite, a halo of dandelion, the dark cloak earthing over your body and helping it come apart.

*

There are deaths we commit to the shape of our names. Blood spilling blood, greed crowding our world. What we take responsibility for, or what we should, the incalculable shape of the suffering wrought.

You could say this death doesn't belong to the greed of our insatiable species. Though one theory might be overpopulation: the elk crowded out of its pastures. This heating up planet. What did the Minnesota woods look like two hundred years ago, stripped of its headlights, unstrangled forest.

Confession

Sometimes I close my eyes and imagine her hands are your hands
sometimes I close my eyes and imagine her hips are your hips

most of the time I keep my eyes open
so I can remember which side
of the veil I am on.

The premise was heartache:
hers, and mine, and the promise
of body pressed up against body
the promise of both of us generating
new skin cells, shucking away
the lovers we'd lost.

The first finding between us was sticky
and hot, streetlamps in summer on Thursday
and at 10:00pm I stopped to stare out the window
and remember the car accident I had not attended
which shattered its way into our lives
at 10:00pm on a Thursday.

Those were early days,
when the hands of her hands
and the hairs of her legs
and the heat lifting off of her body
could pull me most fully into this world
where time travels the length of a long breath,
pleasure and pain operating economy.

Then we both started crying
and laughing
more every time

filling the room with our tangles and broken
filling the room with our wants and our hurts
filling the room with the names of our lost ones
and stitching some kind of net
out of the names.

With her I learned that staying alive might not be
only an act of betrayal
and how many different truths a human can hold
inside of a body at once.

My body is grieving you
harder than my mind or even my heart
it is my body
that wallops and wails for you
whole panels of me shredded away
raw hungering chunks of me ripped
from my flesh

and she comes along to sweet me
and press me to hard me and
soft me and let me undo myself
let me take her into my hands
let me push toward a body
that can push me back
finally doing anything in the operative tense
finally being in charge of anything nothing everything
again

Listen. I choose the world
and you in it. I choose to inhale
this contamination of you
the skin of me still carrying you

the you of her
the me of us
the snarl of this
and love.

I say this very quietly

go looking for the document and who signed their initials.

A series of small confessions
I did
I did not do
I ran away
I did not run
I loved
I could not love enough

I close my eyes and say
the name of every one of your
anatomies—
not a list and not
a prayer: this is a true story.

You had a femur and a mandible.
You had five knuckles
on each of your two hands.
You had valves and capillaries,
you had ball and socket joints
and one long roll of epidermis cloaking
you in light and you
had thousands of small
sprouting hairs.

There was the blood of you beside me
the way your eyes could century what lay before them
the gentle daffodiling of your hair
the swarm of you and your small piles
the way the world fell into you
the way you were the world

I tell this story like a pledge
I give it over quietly and marvel
that you lived and marvel
that you lived and marvel that
you lived

you lived you lived you lived you lived you lived you lived
you lived you lived you lived you lived you lived you lived
you lived you lived you lived you lived you lived you lived
you lived you lived you lived you lived you lived you lived
you lived you lived you lived you lived you lived you lived
you lived you lived you lived you lived you lived you lived
you lived you lived you lived you lived you lived you lived
you lived you lived you lived you lived you lived you lived
you lived you lived you lived you lived you lived you lived
you lived you lived you lived you lived you lived you lived
you lived you lived you lived you lived you lived you lived
you lived you lived you lived you lived you lived you lived
you lived you lived you lived you lived you lived you lived
you lived you lived you lived you lived you lived you lived
you lived you lived you lived you lived you lived you lived
you lived you lived you lived you lived you lived you lived
you lived you lived you lived you lived you lived you lived
you lived you lived you lived you lived you lived you lived
you lived you lived you lived you lived you lived you lived
you lived you lived you lived you lived you lived you lived
you lived you lived you lived you lived you lived you lived
you lived you lived you lived you lived you lived you lived
you lived you lived you lived you lived you lived you lived
you lived you lived you lived you lived you lived you lived
you lived you lived you lived you lived you lived you lived
you lived you lived you lived you lived you lived you lived
you lived you lived you lived you lived you lived you lived
you lived you lived you lived you lived you lived you lived
you lived you lived you lived you lived you lived you lived
you lived you lived you lived you lived you lived you lived
you lived you lived you lived you lived you lived you lived
you lived you lived you lived you lived you lived you lived
you lived you lived you lived you lived you lived you lived
you lived you lived you lived you lived you lived you lived

you lived you lived you lived you lived you lived you lived

you lived.

Visit

When we came upon her she was smiling still, and haloed by the rhythm of lapping. Salt queen, mistress of dark under-places. *This is what death looks like,* you might have said, but you didn't suggest that we sing. We didn't sing, we just watched the unwatchable, the place where a life had been and then drained, something other than seawater leaving the body, the hole in the world was shaped like a porpoise but the world didn't feel any less whole to us. The water was ice at our edges. The sky vaulting over the death.

I keep circling back to this story. There once was a porpoise who cut through the ocean. A muscle, a mammal, a wish in the night. There once were two people who loved one another, who reached for each other until one of them died.

I am not simple,
you told me more than once,
you can't reduce me to a story.

There once was a porpoise, a web of connections, a wet motor whirring within her. She might have been mother, she whimpered in water.

There once were two people who loved one another, who gilded their days in a netting of nicknames. There once were two people who loved one another and tripped over everything while trying to love.

There once was a porpoise and she once had a family and she breathed through her blow-hole and like us, she had lungs.

There once was a boy with all of his needles pointed up to the sky. There once was a girl who walked beside him. There once was a generous world, enough to cup all of them in it. There once was a sky spread wide to hold everything down in its place. There once was an ocean they couldn't see into. There once was a porpoise and there once was a boy and now there is only a girl and a telling.

*

I was trying to learn something about letting go. It was the hardest thing I ever did. I resisted it at every turn. Weeks rolled into months and I was still saying NO to the wall. I was still saying NO to the tallness of trees. Still saying NO to the absence of you. I was digging everything out, shoring you up like a dog and a bone. I was digging you out of your grave every night and moving your limbs around as though you still lived.

*

I was doing it with everyone who ever did it before me. I got dropped into a long sequence of shimmering *no's*. It was an orchestra that wouldn't shut up. I got left behind with the living.

*

Something about what surfaces in a life when trust drops out and the floor of the world is not what we thought it would be.

*

Today is one of those days when everyone is out at the park. There is a festival, it is finally spring. The way people and plants both shore up in the spring. The way they garland their faces in teeth. Today is one of those days. I made myself into a knuckle and sat by the bed. I dug you up and put you back in the bed and sat there watching you. There is so much air-conditioning in the hospital you can almost forget the outside exists. It will always be cold in the hospital. In the summer you lay in the bed and in the autumn you died and now it is spring and it's one of those days but I put you back in the bed so I could avoid all the teeth.

*

When are you coming to see me.

Anger

I wish that I had gone away
for a while. Taken to the seas,
let the wind carve me, the salt.

Rub and abrade away
all my excess. Shucked off
by soft light and hard danger.
Alone on an ocean, to fish
for my dinner and let my insides
turn brined. To be accountable
only to the lapping of waves,
telling time by the swell
and decline of the tide
like the swell and decline of the grief.
The ocean where there are
no false friends, there is
no pretending, the ocean
who holds memory effortlessly
inside her jeweled womb.

To come home later,
unrecognizable. Jaw cut
back by airsalt. Scabbed
and in no way the same.
"You're so different,"
they'd say. I'd say
yes, the storm spat me back.

Confession

have let my softness peel away
and when she picks up
my bones, each one
complete in its curvature
it feels like excavation
like she unearths me from
my regular descent into your grave
I lay to rest in earth mouth, mother
crimson onyx tooth of shale
a nap among the spider roots
a place to be beside you
and then her hand scoops
in deliberate and confident, she
knows what she is digging for
and bone by bone she lifts me
out, patella, femur, rung like
glottis, hook of clavicle
as the soil slips off, the medicine
groans the sour salts ache
she sparks my fingers
to motion, replacing the phalanx
into the hood of its skin
she knows I'm ravenous
to fit her heartbeat inside
my mouth to crawl into
her breathing. I stopped eating
this year so she can find
my bones most easily, collect
them from the earth of you
so she can harvest me when I go under
so I can plant myself beneath the grass
so she can grip me from my hardest parts

when I lay beside you there
she can lift me out again.

Land

To say we grieved your death inseparable from our grieving for the world. This loss is without wall. There isn't world without you, or you without the suffering of everything that touched you. You used to cut apart the seams of paper bags and spread them out across the floor; mapping patterns onto them of earth and sky, names of people and localities, river systems, book titles, watersheds, seed varieties, corporate interests, public schools, holiday seasons, geological processes, extreme weather, marketing trends, patterns of land use, food contamination. There isn't you without this intricacy.

For months I've been reading poems written by the lover to the lost beloved. Poems that are the milk of my days. Sometimes in these poems, loss blasts through the page and context falls away. Sometimes the grief hangs in a suspended position, untouched by what surrounded it. It is life that surrounds both life and death. It is violence that consumes the web, and power that embeds each point of contact between one thing and the next.

You who studied carbon, you who planted fruit trees on sidewalks. The land on which we lost you is a colonized terrain, and it is hard to know exactly how that matters, except that it matters in every single way. This is a story about a boy who died in a world ablaze with destruction and hope. This is a story about a small set of hands joining so many sets of hands in the work of tending to land. And there is no land here without theft and dispossession, there is no way to be here without naming the cost. There is no farming without blood and repentance, there is no mapping that did not teach you complexity. You were embedded on an earth healing itself by the hands of its inheritors who are the children of genociders and the survivors of genocide. Your death is not separate from science or strategy, your death is not separate from battles for water.

The Biggest

What I know of it was clutch and cradle. Many arms moving toward his body at the center. Six sets of arms or seven and six or seven tongues serving song out into the room. And song knitting its thread to song and stitching a bridge of song for him to cross.

What I know of it was all mixed metaphor, time crumbling apart like plaster, gate unlatched and swinging open, the splintering of light against our eyes, his yellow face trembling as his last breaths shook the room, the world, the world inside the room.

It was a learning with no language, a thud and THUD of knowing, just biggest truths arriving into us.

Nobody ever said *he's dying now*, and yet we knew for hours, tethered in by the force of some strong magnet we'll call love for lack of better language, and if I said *intuitive* or if I said *he brought us there* or if I said *he'd been unresponsive for three months and then he called us to his bedside without words*, you might say *right place right time* or you might shrug or you might say *there is so much we do not understand about the brain*.

What I know of it was he who became bird or became timeless as his cells cooled down became royal some kind of beauty too big for me inside. And standing there with him, his heat dropping away, hands folded over hands, eyes hatched for no more drink of light, standing beside his body all that I could say was *it was so generous it was so generous it was a gift it was a gift* it was the biggest gift.

Spring Song

Reverse the peeling apart. Reverse the hush hanging on us. Reverse the way your eyes held me in place when you whispered *you're selfish*. Reverse the last time we lingered. Reverse the last time we touched. Repeat the bright holy bridge strung between our two sets of shoulders.

Reverse shame. Reverse tired. Reverse sleepless nights. Reverse homework. Reverse panic. Reverse dehydration.

Repeat hands quilting skins. Repeat our strange language. Reverse all the ways we fell away from each other.

Reverse silhouettes. Sexism. Scraping the barrel. The times I cringed at your height. The times you spoke me into smallness. Reverse I made you feel guilty. Reverse I made you feel shame. Reverse all the busses, trains, all the highways between us.

Reverse pulp of blame. Reverse gauze of intention. Reverse what went sour and replace it with seashells. Reverse ambiguity.

Replace with some dignified memory of clear steady speech.

Repeat brother, repeat fireplace, repeat season of turning, repeat autumn, and starlight, and songs without words.

Reverse hesitations and stammering tongues. Repeat sitting on a rock and sighting a coyote together.

Strange is the synchronous. Strange is the cusp. Strange was the tilt of me toward you the instant I met you. Strange is the shape of you in front of a campfire the first time I saw you. Strange is the crackle and snap of a fire. *Be safe in the fire,* you said when you blessed me before I got on the plane. Strange is desire, how it disregards rules. Strange is your beard. Strange are your limbs. Strange how I thought I would never.

Reverse all the explaining. Reverse all the pride. Reverse when I told you it wasn't enough. Reverse your wounded ego. Reverse my wounded ambivalence. Reverse all the ways I had already learned not to trust myself by the time that I met you.

Reverse the elk in the road. Reverse the sky over the road. Reverse the slamming together and the slamming apart. Repeat the light pouring out through the whites of your eyes.

Reverse me boarding a plane. Reverse you measuring soil samples. Reverse maps, distances, reverse our ambitions. Reverse all the times I expressed dissatisfaction to other people.

Reverse wounds and withholding. Reverse making excuses. Reverse all the edges of what I'm trying to say.

Reverse that I asked you for solitude and then you gave me solitude. Reverse that I told you to stop crowding me, and then you stopped crowding. Reverse when you went much farther away than I ever meant when I asked.

Reverse I was cold. Reverse you were needy. Reverse all the un-grace that is part of our story. Reverse when you asked me to guard your life through the summer. Reverse how I chose silence and now there is just silence.

Let Go

Let the language fall open
Let the organs exhale
Let the night lift off of its shoulders
Let go taste of copper
Let go humming of blame
29 years is not old is not young.

Let blessings evaporate
Let pencils hit the ground
Let the coyote tongue roll out
slack from the mouth

Let the knees soften
Let the dream ride you
Let the stains of loss fade
into sky

Let go the gray blood
Let go the red mornings
Let the sky come down off of its hooks

Let the sky roll across you like carpet
Let the sky be the mirror of brain
Unclench the unshrinking sky
Let go let go the mad sky

Let the eyes float out over the water
Let the brain spread out
over the sky

Because sky is the inside of your mind
Because sometimes it feels like you gift me the sunset

Let your life fall open and give it
Let the sky take you
Let the sky take the brain
Let it rain brain from the sky
Let go the sky

Elegy

In every book I've read of poems written by the lover to the lost beloved there is a sense of boundedness, a limit-edge, the place where the poems grasp at the confines of what is languageable. A book is a sliver of loss, you can slide it to fit wedged into the blasted-apart place in the heart, but it will never fill the void or speak for the suffering in any sense of completeness. At best a book is a compendium of aches and echoes, of questions and of nouns, somewhere to store them while the sun takes itself to bed in the sky, while the quiet consumes. I wrote this book for you because there was no one else to tell it to, no one who knew to ask or how to listen. Because in losing you I lost my sense of anything to stand on, and I tumbled for a long time. And even as I fell, I was brought closer to everything around me, everything becoming kindred. Everything, and only everything, is big enough to hold us both within it. All of this, like all of you, is the bright and burning name of God. That place where you no longer exist, the wound in the world, is part of the wholeness. The longing thrums at my body, undoes it every day. But the body, like the world, puts herself back together, gathering seed and storing her waters. If the earth should purge herself of us, I will come willingly to you, the praise and the lament of my electric elbows learned from your electric elbows. I have learned that the body heals herself, she learned it from the earth. The darkest pocket of deepest soil that fills your lungs, your mother-tongue. We knew that you were home.

Ars Poetica

Whatever it was
I thought the end of my twenties

would amount to, I was wrong
about that. The end

of my twenties are about
death and the way death drapes

itself sparkling over our lives.
People are falling away

from us, people are peeling
and tumbling away.

The ground calls our names
in its sweet soil voice, the song

of our names rising up
from the ground like the smell

of hot bread lifting
out of its crust.

People are falling away
from us and I have come

to love the darkness of night
like I loved you, like a lover

whose eyes carve me
into the shape of myself

when they look. Everything
extraneous is burning away

but it is not graceful
it is a gift of sharp blade

the end of my twenties
is the surgeon survival

of death cutting back
what I no longer need.

Someone told me to speak
from my scars, not my wounds

which feels true when my body
leans away from the people

whose loved ones
are dying because I am

breathless when death
touches death in the night.

Is a wound too raw
to speak from?

I am sorry
your loved ones are peeling away

but really I
am not sorry.

At the end of my twenties I learned
that one single night can be as long

as a handful of years
that a wound is a story

that stories have names
and when I catalogue it

this night
will bear your name

alongside an index called
Kinds Of Crying, which include:

Ecstatic, Furious, Longing,
Disbelief. Someone told me

to speak from my scars
not my wounds, which might explain why

I am not ready to converse with
the newly bereaved, because

when I bump into them in this long
crackling darkness my wound

heaves its great fist over my
tongue and only my eyes tell

the truth. When I catalogue it
this night will be called The End

Of My Childhood and
it will be called Our Beauty and Terror

it will be called
What We're Here To Do.

I'm not sure though if I agree
about the scars and the wounds

because at the end of my twenties
it is my hand reaching

into the mouth of the wound
to pull forth each word

to place it against the blank page
where it cools and solidifies

and isn't that maybe the way a scar
forms? And the sweet song

of the earth
beckoning

all of us
back.

Gratitude

To Gabe Adels, Sam Adels, Stacey Meadows, Peter Adels, Claire Briguglio, Steven Winokur and Cristoph Spath; an intimate and profound gratitude that extends far beyond language ever could. You have my heart.

Additionally, my deepest thanks go to: Adam Deutsch and the team at Cooper Dillon Books for encouraging the creation of this book with warmth, generosity, skill and deep attention. Lillian-Yvonne Bertram and Manuel Paul López for the great blessings of your reading. Stevie Edwards, KMA Sullivan, and the staff of YesYes Books, for also wanting and bringing these words into the world so lovingly. Aurora Levins-Morales and Sasha Warner-Berry for your tremendous editorial skills, abundance of time and care; for nursing this book into existence. Merle Feld, Tessa Landreau-Grasmuck, Clay Muwin River, and MJ Kaufman, for reading many versions of these poems, for invaluable feedback and kinship. Jill Magi, Jen Hofer, and Rick Benjamin, for teaching me to write. Beth Naditch, Julie Leavitt, Jennileen Joseph, and Sharon Cohen-Anisfeld, the mentors and healers who tended my broken heart and taught me to spin it to light. Ilana Lerman, Beth Blum, Vivian Lehrer, Rachel Sibley, and Marina Weisz, who particularly kept me alive in the darkest years. The Ruskin-Fornaris, Fishman-Braunigs, and to RayRay Farrales and Leora Abelson, for home. To Jess Benjamin for so much patience. To my family: Daniel Gomery, Dina Gomery, Pablo Gomery, and Elena Rath Goldstein, for an unconditional love that sustains me. To my ancestors whose words run through me.

There are many more people who are woven into the creation of this book in ways that I do and don't understand. To write a comprehensive list feels impossible. Thank you —friends, classmates, teachers, neighbors. Without you I could not have written these, or any, poems.

And finally, to Jonah, for whom this book is written. A wild and enduring love, a gratitude of many lifetimes. *In your light we see light.*

Mónica Gomery is a rabbi and poet, raised by her Venezuelan Jewish family in Boston and Caracas, and now living in Philadelphia. Her work explores queerness, diaspora, ancestry, theology, and cultivating courageous hearts. She is a graduate of the Creative Writing BFA program at Goddard College and received rabbinic ordination from Hebrew College. She is the author of the poetry collection *Here is the Night and the Night on the Road (Cooper Dillon Books, 2018)*, and the chapbook *Of Darkness and Tumbling* (YesYes Books, 2017). She is the winner of the 2020 Minola Review Poetry Contest, judged by Doyali Islam, and has been a Pushcart Prize nominee, and a finalist in the Cutthroat Journal Joy Harjo Poetry Contest. Her writing has appeared in numerous journals and publications. *Here is the Night and the Night on the Road* is her first full-length book of poetry. She lives in Philadelphia, on unceded Lenni Lenape land, with her partner and her dog.

www.ingramcontent.com/pod-product-compliance
Lightning Source LLC
Chambersburg PA
CBHW021443080526
44588CB00009B/672